GRIEF
Living at Peace with Loss

JUNE HUNT

ROSE PUBLISHING/ASPIRE PRESS

Torrance, California

ROSE PUBLISHING/ASPIRE PRESS

Grief: Living at Peace with Loss
Copyright © 2013 Hope For The Heart
All rights reserved.
Aspire Press, a division of Rose Publishing, Inc.
4733 Torrance Blvd., #259
Torrance, California 90503 USA
www.aspirepress.com

Register your book at www.aspirepress.com/register
Get inspiration via email, sign up at www.aspirepress.com

Printed in the United States of America
030214DP

CONTENTS

Dear friend,

I know what it's like to feel intense grief—a penetrating grief that cannot be escaped or denied. I also know about *unexpected grief*—those times when grief catches me off guard, particularly when "out of the blue" a painful memory floods my mind, raining tears upon my soul.

How well I remember traveling to Indiana to speak at a conference that began with a buffet dinner. As I was standing in line, I noticed a younger woman attentively serving the plate of an older woman with a walker. I couldn't help but notice the tender affection between this mother and daughter. Immediately, a wave of grief swept over me. Tears filled my eyes. I quickly left the room. I cried.

Simply put, that mother/daughter scene evoked precious memories of my mother and me, my mother who, just four weeks before, we buried. Never again would I have the privilege of serving her, seating her, sitting with her. Never again could I hug her, kiss her, hold her. Oh, how I missed her.

Unexpected grief can occur anytime and anyplace, especially when we see something that reminds us of someone dear to our hearts—someone no longer in our lives.

Grief finds us at unexpected times, like the time I walked into a card shop, saw a bird's nest, and all of a sudden, felt my eyes fill with tears. I had to turn and walk out of the store. Again, that familiar wave of grief flooded my soul. Although many months had passed since my mother's death, the moment I saw the bird's nest, I thought of her. She loved what the nest represents: security, family, intimacy. Once for Mother's Day, I designed a bracelet for her that contained the birthstones of my three siblings and me closely nestled together inside a gold nest. Whenever I found a bird's nest (which was rare), I would get it for her and she would be utterly delighted. That day, in that card shop, I had found another endearing nest—but it was too late. The time had passed, and my heart grieved.

Periodically you, like me, will go through seasons of grief. After you lose someone or something immensely meaningful, you need to *expect moments of unexpected grief.*

No matter the heartache, realize that God is with you in the midst of your grief. And when you allow Jesus Christ to have control of your life, you can truly live at peace with your loss.

Yours in the Lord's hope,

June

June Hunt

"Weeping may remain for a night,
but rejoicing comes in the morning."
(Psalm 30:5)

GRIEF
Living at Peace with Loss

Why are people so drawn to Jesus, especially when their hearts have lost all hope? Why do they assume He will sympathize with their sorrows? Why would He grieve over their griefs? The answer is simple: Jesus was no stranger to grief. He was slandered and scourged, belittled and beaten, criticized and crucified. Yet the Bible says,

> "When they hurled their insults at him,
> he did not retaliate;
> when he suffered, he made no threats.
> Instead, he entrusted himself
> to him who judges justly."
> (1 Peter 2:23)

When you see someone being insulted, when you hear someone being slandered, when you watch someone suffering, you know that person not only *understands grief,* but also *feels grief.* When Jesus lived on earth, His onlookers saw the unjust insults hurled at Him, heard the unjust slander spoken of Him, watched the unjust suffering imposed on Him. Therefore, they knew He was one who could both understand their grief and care about their grief.

▶ If you feel, "No one cares about my pain"— Jesus cares!

▶ If you think, "No one cares about my sorrow"—Jesus cares!

▶ If you believe, "No one cares about my grief"—Jesus cares!

*"Casting all your care upon him,
for he cares for you."* (1 Peter 5:7 NKJV)

People are drawn to Jesus because Jesus cares, and that is why you too can turn to Him.

"We do not have a high priest
who is unable to sympathize
with our weaknesses,
but we have one
who has been tempted
in every way, just as we are—
yet was without sin.
Let us then approach
the throne of grace with confidence,
so that we may receive mercy
and find grace to help us
in our time of need."
(Hebrews 4:15–17)

DEFINITIONS OF GRIEF

Who has not questioned the reason for pain and suffering in the world? Certainly some people have become hardened by their losses, while others have become softened; God used their grief to cultivate in them tender, understanding hearts.

Only days before His own death, Jesus traveled to the grave of Lazarus to comfort his two sisters in their loss. Jesus was not only *deeply moved in His Spirit*, but He was also weeping with Mary and Martha. It may seem paradoxical that Jesus—the Son of God, the one who turned water into wine, the one who multiplied the loaves and the fishes, the one who raised Lazarus from the dead—could not avoid grief in His own life. But the prophet Isaiah foretold that Christ, the coming Messiah, would be a man who would understand grief well for, indeed, He was ...

> "A Man of sorrows
> and acquainted with grief."
> (Isaiah 53:3 NKJV)

▶ *Grief* is the painful emotion of sorrow caused by the loss or impending loss of anyone or anything that has deep meaning to you.

"Be merciful to me, O Lord, for I am in distress; my eyes grow weak with sorrow, my soul and my body with grief." (Psalm 31:9)

▶ *Grief* begins in your heart as a natural response to a significant, unwanted loss.

▶ *Grief* is a God-given emotion that increases with knowledge about the sorrows of life. The wiser you are about the grief that people experience, the more you yourself will grieve.[1]

"With much wisdom comes much sorrow; the more knowledge, the more grief." (Ecclesiastes 1:18)

▶ In the New Testament, the Greek word *lupe* means "pain of body or mind."[2] When Jesus told His disciples He would soon be betrayed and killed, they were *"filled with grief"* (Matthew 17:23).

▶ *Mourning* (also called grieving), is the process of working through the pain of sorrow that follows a significant loss.

"Joy is gone from our hearts; our dancing has turned to mourning." (Lamentations 5:15)

▶ *Mourning* is a normal, healthy process that lasts for a period of time. God uses mourning in order to produce the ultimate healing of deep distress and sorrow.

"You turned my wailing into dancing; you removed my sackcloth and clothed me with joy." (Psalm 30:11)

▶ *Mourning* evokes compassion and expressions of comfort from others. When Lazarus died, Jesus and many others came to comfort Mary and Martha.

"Many Jews had come to Martha and Mary to comfort them in the loss of their brother." (John 11:19)

In the Old Testament, the Hebrew word *abal* means "to mourn or lament."[3] Jacob's favorite son was Joseph. When Joseph's brothers told their father, Jacob, that his favored son had been killed by a ferocious animal, Jacob went into deep mourning for days and ultimately years.

"Jacob tore his clothes, put on sackcloth and mourned for his son many days." (Genesis 37:34)

WHAT IS Chronic Grief?

While we are grieving, a prevalent problem may be that we don't want to talk about our grief or let others see our sadness. We don't want to appear weak, so we mask our emotions! Yet if we delay sharing our sorrow, our healing will also be delayed. If we are going to be "authentically human," we need to be able to share the truth about the heaviness in our hearts. If we have chronic grief, we are emotionally stuck, and we need to be set free. That is why Jesus' words about truth are so freeing, even when applied to grieving.

> **"You will know the truth,
> and the truth will set you free."
> (John 8:32)**

▶ *Chronic grief* (or incomplete grief) is an unresolved, emotional sorrow experienced over a long period of time as the result of not accepting a significant loss or not experiencing closure of that loss.[4]

"The troubles of my heart have multiplied; free me from my anguish." (Psalm 25:17)

▶ *Chronic grief* can also be an unresolved, deep sorrow experienced over a long period of time and characterized by misconceptions that result in a failure to move through the grief process.

MISCONCEPTION: "My grief will never end."

CORRECTION: You will mourn for a season, and then your grief will end.

"[There is] a time to mourn and a time to dance." (Ecclesiastes 3:4)

MISCONCEPTION: "If I cry, I'm not strong."

CORRECTION: Jesus was strong, yet He wept after Lazarus died.

"Jesus wept." (John 11:35)

King David was strong, yet he and his men wept after Saul and Jonathan died.

"They mourned and wept and fasted till evening for Saul and his son Jonathan." (2 Samuel 1:12)

MISCONCEPTION: "If I feel deep sorrow, I must not be trusting God."

CORRECTION: Christ, the Messiah, never failed to trust God, the Father, yet He was called *"a man of sorrows."*

"He was despised and rejected by men, a man of sorrows, and familiar with suffering." (Isaiah 53:3)

Have you seen someone smiling, yet within the smile you recognized sadness? Have you heard someone laughing, though you knew the heart was not healed? This is a picture of "repressed grief."

> "Even in laughter the heart may ache,
> and joy may end in grief."
> (Proverbs 14:13)

Repressed grief occurs when a person has reason to grieve and needs to grieve, but does not grieve.[5]

The person with repressed grief exhibits negative lifestyle patterns but does not know why. (Examples may be distancing from others, playing the clown, using mood-altering substances like alcohol or drugs, engaging in mood-altering behaviors like gambling, or compulsive spending).

Only by facing the truth of your painful losses in life and by going through genuine grief will you have emotional healing.

In the Bible, the Psalmist prayed this prayer:

> "Send forth your light and your truth,
> let them guide me."
> (Psalm 43:3)

The Timeline Test

Repressed grief can be overcome and grieving can begin when a person takes **The Timeline Test**.[6]

▶ **Draw** a long, horizontal line representing your life.

▶ **Divide** the timeline into three sections—childhood, youth, and adulthood.

▶ **Denote** the major changes in your life. Draw short lines extending from the timeline and write short phrases by each line that describe all significant events, such as:

- birth of siblings
- change of school
- death of loved ones/pets
- lost friendships
- abuse (verbal, emotional, physical, sexual)
- broken engagement
- abortion
- marriage
- relocation
- miscarriage
- childlessness, infertility
- "empty nest," children leaving the home or marriage of children
- separation/divorce
- job loss/new job
- illnesses/injuries
- financial loss
- retirement

▶ **Determine** whether there are any sad experiences or significant losses and hurts over which you have never grieved or have never finished grieving, such as:

- abandonment
- rejection
- divorce of parents
- unmet goals
- failures
- unjust criticism
- false accusations
- unrealized dreams

▶ **Discover** the source of your masked pain through earnest prayer.

▶ **Define** the painful events over which you need to grieve by using specific statements.

- "I am grieving over ... "
- "I was so embarrassed when ... "
- "I felt abandoned by ... "
- "I was really hurt when ... "
- "I've been determined to never let (_____) happen again."

▶ **Decide** *now* to allow deep genuine grieving over your losses.

> "Heal me, O Lord,
> and I will be healed;
> save me and I will be saved,
> for you are the one I praise."
> (Jeremiah 17:14)

▶ **Defuse** the power these events have over your emotions by sharing your feelings with a trusted person and with God.

"There is a time ... to speak."
(Ecclesiastes 3:1, 7)

▶ **Deepen** your dependence on the Lord to set you emotionally free.

"In my anguish I cried to the LORD,
and he answered by setting me free."
(Psalm 118:5)

PRAYER FOR DISCOVERY

*"Oh, Father, I come to You
as Your child for help. Calm my heart.
Enable me to see what I need to see. Make
me aware of my need for healing and
show me Your truth.
Bring to my mind any buried pain. . . .
Surface any hidden hurt and the exact
circumstances that caused it.
I ask You to help my wounded heart to
heal. I know You have the power to make
me whole. I am willing to face whatever
You want me to face
so that I can be set free.
In Your holy name, I pray, Amen."*

Example: *My Timeline*

Life Stages	Age	Events
Childhood		Birth
	1	Father abandons family, parents divorce
	5	Mother remarries, stepfather abuses
	6	Starts school, brother born
	8	Moves to new city, new school
	10	Moves again, new school but no friends
Youth	13	Starts junior high school
	15	Moves to new house
	17	Graduates from high school
	17	Cousin is killed in auto accident
	18	Grandmother dies (only person I could count on), begins college

Life Stages	Age	Events
Adulthood	19	Marries to leave home, daughter born
	22	Pregnant, husband leaves, son born
	23	Divorces, runs away, new job, new city
	25	Attempts suicide
	27	Remarries, father and two uncles die
	31	Accepts Christ as Savior
	37	Daughter graduates, goes to college
	42	Daughter returns pregnant but unmarried
	43	Becomes a grandmother
	45	Son graduates, daughter marries, empty nest
	48	New job, new career
	52	Husband loses business of 20 years
	52	Mother moves in with us
	53	Lose our home, more financial problems
	55	Mother dies (best friend)

WHAT IS "Grief Work"?

Do you feel that your grief will never end, that your loss is a continual source of sorrow? Moving through the grief process takes time and commitment to "stay the course" until the goal of grief is accomplished. Working through your grief is not an easy task; it is a difficult task that involves dedication. Be assured, God has a plan for you during this season of pain, and God will give you the strength to persevere through the pain.

> "You need to persevere so that when you have done the will of God, you will receive what he has promised."
> (Hebrews 10:36)

▶ Grief work involves a step-by-step process through which a grieving person walks in order to reach a place of emotional healing.[7]

"Though I walk in the midst of trouble, you preserve my life." (Psalm 138:7)

▶ Healthy grief work will culminate in:[8]

- *accepting* that the past will always be in the past

- *accepting* that the present offers stability and significance

- *accepting* that the future holds new and promising hope

In the end you can say, along with the apostle Paul ...

"We also rejoice in our sufferings,
because we know that suffering
produces perseverance;
perseverance, character;
and character, hope.
And hope does not disappoint us,
because God has poured out his love
into our hearts by the Holy Spirit,
whom he has given us."
(Romans 5:3–5)

CHARACTERISTICS

"We don't want to hear it! We don't believe it! We won't accept it!" While Jesus' disciples didn't speak these words literally, these sentiments resounded in the hearts of His followers—especially Peter. The shock, confusion, and fear of Christ's impending death seemed too great to comprehend. In John 16:18 they protested, *"We don't understand what he is saying."* Despite their grief, Jesus persisted in telling them the truth. He loved His disciples too much to enable their denial.

Grief over the death of a significant person in your life doesn't just go away in a few days, weeks, or months. Healthy grieving can last for one, two, or even five years.[9] This is especially true with the loss of a beloved child, parent, or mate. Everyone grieves differently, but everyone must grieve in order to heal. As you entrust yourself to the Lord, your grieving gradually lessens and He restores joy to your heart. And, someday, if not in this life, then in the life to come—like the disciples—you will understand how God can take even the most unspeakable losses and turn them to joy.

> **"You will grieve,**
> **but your grief will turn to joy."**
> **(John 16:20)**

When we initially experience a significant loss, we can plunge into depths of grief and have difficulty coming up for air. Then eventually, after we surface, we are simply treading water, not swimming toward a real destination. The reason is called *grief*. When you feel engulfed with grief, realize that you have a Deliverer who will keep you from drowning in the depths of despair.

> "He reached down from on high
> and took hold of me;
> he drew me out of deep waters."
> (Psalm 18:16)

☐ Do you feel alone and isolated?

☐ Do you feel that you are mechanically going through the motions of life?

☐ Do you feel resentful toward God for allowing your loss?

☐ Do you ask, "*Why?*" over and over again?

☐ Do you feel overwhelmed, not knowing what to do or where to turn?

☐ Do you feel emotionally distraught because of your loss?

☐ Do you have frequent daydreams about your loss?

☐ Do you feel angry or bitter over your loss?

☐ Do you have difficulty forgiving those who caused your loss?

☐ Do you frequently dream at night about your loss?

☐ Do you see life as an empty struggle without much reward?

☐ Do you feel helpless knowing how much others must also be suffering?

☐ Do you wonder what kind of God would allow your loss?

☐ Do you view God as uninvolved and lacking compassion?

Regardless of your view of God right now, the Bible says ...

"The Lord is good, a refuge
in times of trouble.
He cares for those who trust in him."
(Nahum 1:7)

Allowing yourself to be open and honest about your intense sorrow takes great courage.[10] For some, the reality of personal pain has been buried so deeply that the ability to experience real grief is blocked. People do many things to camouflage or ignore their grief so that they don't have to acknowledge and work through it. As a result, they have unhealthy, chronic grief, which is a barrier to emotional maturity. This unresolved sorrow blocks the comfort that Christ wants to give us. In the Beatitudes Jesus said ...

> **"Blessed are those who mourn, for they will be comforted." (Matthew 5:4)**

▶ *Inhibited* grief – denial of grief

"This is not really happening to me."

▶ *Isolated* grief – selective remembering

"I refuse to think about that car accident again."

▶ *Insulated* grief – reduced emotional involvement

"I'm not going to open myself up to be hurt this way again."

▶ *Intellectualized* grief – rationally explaining events

"It could have been worse."

▶ *Inverted* grief – returning to immature ways of responding

"I can't believe it! I just had a temper tantrum like one I had when I was five years old."

▶ *Immortalized* grief – inability to let go of the loss

"He will always be a part of everything in my life."

WHAT ARE the Stages of Healthy Grieving?

Emotional complications occur when we block the natural process of grieving.[11] Have you ever told yourself, *I need to get my act together. I've got to snap out of it. I should be handling this better!* These self-incriminating thoughts reveal unrealistic expectations about grieving and a failure to understand the grief process and the slow journey of restoration.

While "stages" of grief do exist, they are not "stair-step" stages that you walk through in a specific order. In truth, people do not go through all the stages in a predictable fashion. People are unique in their individual grieving.

Some stages may be experienced with varying degrees of intensity, some may be missed, and some stages may be repeated. Give yourself permission to experience the inconsistent stages of grieving, trusting God to bring new life again.

> **"Though you have made me see troubles, many and bitter, you will restore my life again; from the depths of the earth you will again bring me up."**
> **(Psalm 71:20)**

▶ *Crisis Stage*

This stage can last from two days to two weeks. In this stage of grief, you are mechanically going through daily activities. You will experience many of the following characteristics:

- anxiety/fear
- appetite/sleep loss
- concentration limited
- confusion
- crying uncontrollably
- denial
- disturbing dreams
- exhaustion
- feeling trapped
- shock/numbness

"My eyes will flow unceasingly, without relief."
(Lamentations 3:49)

▶ *Crucible Stage*

This stage can last up to a year or two or more, perhaps even until death if grief is not resolved. This time of sorrow will be accompanied by many of the following characteristics:

- anger/resentment

- anguish

- appetite/sleep loss

- bargaining with God

- depression/sadness

- guilt/false guilt

- helplessness/lethargy

- judgment impaired

- loneliness/isolation

- low self-worth

- self-pity/victim mentality

- intense yearning

"My soul is in anguish. How long, O Lord, how long?" (Psalm 6:3)

▶ *Contentment Stage*

This stage accepts the loss, leaving it in the past. This stage not only accepts that the present offers stability, but also accepts that the future offers new and promising hope. As this time approaches, the following characteristics may become more and more apparent.

- greater compassion toward others
- greater acceptance of others
- greater appreciation of others
- greater humility before others
- greater dependence on the Lord
- a new ability to leave the loss behind
- new patterns for living
- new purpose in life
- new hope for the future
- new contentment in all circumstances

"One thing I do: Forgetting what is behind and straining toward what is ahead. ... For I have learned to be content whatever the circumstances." (Philippians 3:13; 4:11)

When your heart breaks over a great loss, intense grief will touch every aspect of your life—your body, soul, and spirit. The effects of this intense grief will vary in degree, ranging from mild to severe, depending on where you are in the grieving process. While you will not experience all the effects, everyone will experience some of them. Realize that these effects are common to everyone who grieves and are temporary as long as you face the pain of your loss and work through the grief process.

In the Psalms, David recounts both the bitterness of his grief and the assurance of God's presence.

> "When my heart was grieved
> and my spirit embittered,
> I was senseless and ignorant;
> I was a brute beast before you.
> Yet I am always with you;
> you hold me by my right hand.
> You guide me with your counsel,
> and afterward you will
> take me into glory."
> (Psalm 73:21–24)

Physical effects:

- exhaustion
- headaches
- inability to sleep
- indigestion
- loss of appetite
- stress-induced illnesses

Emotional/mental effects:

- depression and anxiety
- dreams about the deceased
- forgetfulness and disorganization
- guilt and anger
- loneliness and withdrawal
- threats of self-destruction/suicide

Social effects:

- antisocial behavior
- awkwardness
- escape behaviors (excessive drinking, drugs, travel, gambling, sex)
- excessive busyness
- tensions in existing relationships
- withdrawal

Spiritual effects:

- anger at God
- doubting the love, fairness, and faithfulness of God
- fear of God and dread about the future
- inability to pray or read the Bible
- withdrawal from spiritual activities
- questions about why God allowed the loss

> "Why is life given to a man
> whose way is hidden,
> whom God has hedged in?
> For sighing comes to me
> instead of food;
> my groans pour out like water.
> What I feared has come upon me;
> what I dreaded has happened to me.
> I have no peace, no quietness;
> I have no rest, but only turmoil."
> (Job 3:23–26)

CAUSES OF GRIEF

Imagine if there had been a number of heartless murders of multiple newborn babies, infants, and toddlers in your hometown. How would you feel? Imagine that you knew many of their parents. Would they not be grief stricken? Would their hearts not be crushed and their dreams shattered? Now, imagine that throughout your life you knew that *you were the baby targeted for destruction*—not the others, yet you escaped (See Matthew chapter 2). No wonder Jesus had great compassion for those who grieved! No wonder He could sympathize with their sorrows.

When King Herod heard the wise men ask, *"Where is the one who has been born King of the Jews?"* (Matthew 2:2), he reacted in fear that this up-and-coming king would be a threat to his throne. As a result, Herod plotted to kill all the baby boys in Judea—and kill them he did! But Herod's plan did not trump God's plan. For indeed King Herod died while King Jesus lived. And today, in spite of your deepest trials and trouble, if you are an authentic believer in the Lord Jesus Christ, He lives in your heart to give you His peace. Jesus said ...

"In me you may have peace. In this world you will have trouble. But take heart! I have overcome the world." (John 16:33)

Everyone has been created with three God-given inner needs—the needs for love, for significance, and for security.[12] When one or more of these needs is no longer being met, we naturally feel a sense of loss, which in turn causes grief.

Unmet need → Sense of loss → Feeling of grief

Throughout our lives we will incur numerous losses. Although we need to feel the pain of our losses, we do not need to be controlled by our losses. Instead we must rely on God's promise that He will meet our deepest inner needs.

The Bible says ...

> "My God will meet all your needs
> according to his glorious riches
> in Christ Jesus."
> (Philippians 4:19)

▶ Loss of Love

- loss of significant family member (spouse, parent, unborn baby, child)

- loss of an endeared pet

- loss of a romantic relationship

- loss of ability to have children (childlessness, infertility)

- loss of a close friend

- loss of an admired mentor or role model

Great Trial: "I'm still in agony over the death of my husband, and I feel like I'm only half a person."

God's Truth: Take comfort in this. Although your loss is severe and even though you have no earthly husband, the Lord says He will be your husband—He will be your Provider and Protector.

"For your Maker is your husband—the LORD Almighty is his name." (Isaiah 54:5)

▶ **Loss of Significance**

- loss of employment

- loss of hopes and dreams

- loss of freedom

- loss of achievement

- loss of respect/reputation

- loss of purpose

Great Trial: "I've lost everything that gives my life purpose, and I feel such a sense of loss."

God's Truth: Take comfort in this. As long as you are alive, your life has purpose.

"The LORD will fulfill his purpose for me; your love, O LORD, endures forever." (Psalm 138:8)

▶ Loss of Security

- loss of companionship
- loss of health (physical abilities)
- loss of finances
- loss of home
- loss of justice
- loss of family environment

Great Trial: "I've just experienced the greatest rejection of my life, and I feel overwhelmed with grief."

God's Truth: Take comfort in this. While people reject people, the Lord will not reject you. He says,

"I have chosen you and have not rejected you. So do not fear, for I am with you; do not be dismayed, for I am your God. I will strengthen you and help you; I will uphold you with my righteous right hand." (Isaiah 41:9–10)

Like favorite folk remedies for a winter cold, solutions for overcoming grief are numerous and seem to be offered by everyone. When grieving a loss, you can expect to receive plenty of advice, especially from well-intentioned family and friends valiantly seeking to help you overcome your pain. Unfortunately, the advice is often as conflicting as it is plentiful and may leave you feeling as though you will never find a way to lessen your pain. However, even when your heart seems heaviest, God promises to be your light, breaking through the darkest night of your soul with tender comfort. If you entrust your life to the Lord, He will instruct you, teach you, and guide you every step of the way.

> "Show me your ways, O LORD,
> teach me your paths;
> guide me in your truth and teach me,
> for you are God my Savior,
> and my hope is in you all day long."
> (Psalm 25:4–5)

Common Misconceptions about Mourning[13]

FALLACY:

"Mourners need to become busy and laugh a lot in order to keep from thinking about their loss."

FACT:

While it is helpful for those who are grieving to be productive in mental and physical activities and to laugh when it is natural, ignoring their loss is counterproductive. They need both to face and to feel their grief. The Bible illustrates this point graphically.

"Like one who takes away a garment on a cold day, or like vinegar poured on soda, is one who sings songs to a heavy heart." (Proverbs 25:20)

FALLACY:

"Mourners need to move to a new home as soon as possible and focus on finding pleasure."

FACT:

Following the death of a loved one who lived at home, consider this as a general rule: make no major changes for one to two years. Moving to a different home may be appropriate, but only for the right reason at the right time. Before making a major decision like moving, ask the Lord for wisdom—He will provide.

"If any of you lacks wisdom, he should ask God, who gives generously to all without finding fault, and it will be given to him." (James 1:5)

FALLACY:

"Mourners should keep their grief to themselves."

FACT:

Keeping your grief away from others is like keeping the sick away from medical aid—it keeps those grieving away from those who could give comfort, help, and healing. The Bible says we are to ...

"Mourn with those who mourn."
(Romans 12:15)

FALLACY:

"Mourning is primarily relegated to women, not to men."

FACT:

While all cultures have their own male and female stereotypes, grief is not related to gender, but rather to people. Grief impacts men and women alike, although they may express their grief in different ways. Certainly men grieve too. For example, when Stephen, the first Christian martyr, was stoned to death, the Bible says ...

"Godly men buried Stephen and mourned deeply for him." (Acts 8:2)

FALLACY:

"If you love someone, you should grieve forever."

FACT:

You can love forever, but you don't have to grieve forever. How honorably you live, not how long you grieve, gives the greatest tribute to your loved one. Grieving has a definite beginning, and through God, it can have a definite ending. In a poetic way, David described how his grieving came to an end.

"You, O Lord, have delivered my soul from death, my eyes from tears, my feet from stumbling." (Psalm 116:8)

FALLACY:

"Mourners need a major change in their lifestyles."

FACT:

Self-imposed, radical changes will only add to present stress and cause greater insecurity. In time, the desire for certain changes will come and beneficial change will take place when the time is right.

"There is a proper time and procedure for every matter, though a man's misery weighs heavily upon him." (Ecclesiastes 8:6)

Sometimes God allows you to experience deep grief and suffering as a means of bringing about godly results in your life.

> "See now that I myself am He! There is no god besides me. I put to death and I bring to life, I have wounded and I will heal, and no one can deliver out of my hand." (Deuteronomy 32:39)

▶ **In His sovereignty, God allows evil, grief, and suffering through:**

- **The free will of every human being** (to make choices, which in turn, can cause suffering)

  "Do not be deceived: God cannot be mocked. A man reaps what he sows. The one who sows to please his sinful nature, from that nature will reap destruction; the one who sows to please the Spirit, from the Spirit will reap eternal life." (Galatians 6:7–8)

- **The acts of nature** (earthquakes and other natural disasters)

  "Then a great and powerful wind tore the mountains apart and shattered the rocks before the LORD, but the LORD was not in the wind. After the wind there was an earthquake, but the LORD was not in the earthquake." (1 Kings 19:11)

▶ **In His sovereignty, God can use grief and suffering to:**[14]

- **Produce perseverance, character, and hope in you**

  "We also rejoice in our sufferings, because we know that suffering produces perseverance; perseverance, character; and character, hope. And hope does not disappoint us, because God has poured out his love into our hearts by the Holy Spirit, whom he has given us." (Romans 5:3–5)

- **Save souls**

  "You intended to harm me, but God intended it for good to accomplish what is now being done, the saving of many lives." (Genesis 50:20)

- **Develop dependence on Him**

  "The widow who is really in need and left all alone puts her hope in God and continues night and day to pray and to ask God for help." (1 Timothy 5:5)

- **Cause crying out to Him**

  "I cry aloud to the LORD; I lift my voice to the LORD for mercy, I pour out my complaint before him; before him I tell my trouble. When my spirit grows faint within me, it is you who know my way." (Psalm 142:1–3)

- **Humble your heart**

  "Remember how the LORD your God led you all the way in the desert these forty years, to humble you and to test you in order to know what was in your heart, whether or not you would keep his commands." (Deuteronomy 8:2)

- **Further your faith**

  "These have come so that your faith—of greater worth than gold, which perishes even though refined by fire—may be proved genuine and may result in praise, glory and honor when Jesus Christ is revealed." (1 Peter 1:7)

- **Show His strength in your weaknesses**

  "I [Paul] delight in weaknesses, in insults, in hardships, in persecutions, in difficulties. For when I am weak, then I am strong." (2 Corinthians 12:10)

- **Cause you to share Christ's sufferings**

  "Dear friends, do not be surprised at the painful trial you are suffering, as though something strange were happening to you. But rejoice that you participate in the sufferings of Christ, so that you may be overjoyed when his glory is revealed." (1 Peter 4:12–13)

- **Reveal His heart**

"Those who suffer he delivers in their suffering; he speaks to them in their affliction." (Job 36:15)

- **Teach and train**

"No discipline seems pleasant at the time, but painful. Later on, however, it produces a harvest of righteousness and peace for those who have been trained by it." (Hebrews 12:11)

- **Conform you to Christlikeness**

"For it is commendable if a man bears up under the pain of unjust suffering because he is conscious of God. But how is it to your credit if you receive a beating for doing wrong and endure it? But if you suffer for doing good and you endure it, this is commendable before God. To this you were called, because Christ suffered for you, leaving you an example, that you should follow in his steps." (1 Peter 2:19–21)

- **Extend Christ's comfort**

"[He] comforts us in all our troubles, so that we can comfort those in any trouble with the comfort we ourselves have received from God." (2 Corinthians 1:4)

So many times grief and guilt walk hand in hand. When we are in the throes of guilt, it is not uncommon for us to lament, *If only I had ... I should have ... Why didn't I ... !* The problem is that sometimes we can't distinguish whether we are grappling with false guilt or true guilt. We need to be able to discern the difference.

False Guilt

The following question is an example of a situation in which a grieving person found herself unknowingly feeling *false* guilt.

QUESTION: "My sister died unexpectedly of a heart attack. How can I ever forgive myself for not being there for her in her time of need?"

ANSWER: Obviously, you would have done everything in your power to have saved your sister's life. But saving her life was not in your power. In truth, you are struggling with false guilt.

▶ False guilt arises when you blame yourself, even though you have committed no wrong, or when you continue to blame yourself after you have confessed and turned from your sin.

▶ False guilt is resolved by recognizing the lie you have believed and by refusing to accept it. Then acknowledge the truth and accept it instead.

In His sovereignty, God has numbered each of our days, and you were not granted power to alter His plan. Clearly, you have a God-ordained season of grieving before you, but don't grieve because of the pain of false guilt. Grieve because of the loss of your beloved sister.

"Man's days are determined; you have decreed the number of his months and have set limits he cannot exceed." (Job 14:5)

True Guilt

The following question is an example of a situation in which a grieving person found himself genuinely feeling *true* guilt.

QUESTION: "I'm truly grieving. I made a series of bad choices that involved placing money as a higher priority than my wife. Now she has left me. What can I do?"

ANSWER: When you know you've been in the habit of "majoring on the minors," you have choices. Typically, we learn *painful* lessons well! Because you have *brought this grief upon yourself,* plan now to change your priorities. Replace your bad decisions with these good decisions.

▶ Evaluate what you did wrong.

▶ Genuinely repent.

▶ Admit to her that you were wrong and ask for her forgiveness.

▶ Then live your life "majoring on the majors."

Do not pressure her. She will see for herself whether you have really changed from focusing on money to focusing on maturity.

"The love of money is a root of all kinds of evil. Some people, eager for money, have wandered from the faith and pierced themselves with many griefs." (1 Timothy 6:10)

HOW DO You Resolve the Grief Caused by True Guilt?

We've all been wrong. We've all been guilty. We've all violated the will of God, going against what His Word tells us.

God created us with an innate need to have a loving relationship with Him. But when we go against His will, a wall is erected between us and God—a spiritual barricade. This wall is called sin. Sin is choosing to go our own way instead of God's way and, therefore, results in true guilt.

"Here we are before you in our guilt, though because of it not one of us can stand in your presence." (Ezra 9:15)

How Can You Find God's Forgiveness and Live Guilt-Free?

The Four Points of God's Plan

You can understand God's solution for you by reading His Word. His plan can be spelled out in four simple points.

#1 God's Purpose for You is *Salvation*.

What was God's motive in sending Christ to earth?

To condemn you? No, to express His love for you by saving you!

"For God so loved the world that he gave his one and only Son, that whoever believes in him shall not perish but have eternal life. For God did not send his Son into the world to condemn the world, but to save the world through him." (John 3:16–17)

What was Jesus' purpose in coming to earth? To make everything perfect and to remove all sin, guilt, and grief?

No, to forgive your sins, empower you to have victory over sin, and enable you to live a fulfilled life without the grief of guilt!

"I [Jesus] have come that they may have life, and have it to the full." (John 10:10)

#2 Your Problem is *Sin.*

What exactly is sin?

Sin is living *independently* of God's standard—knowing what is right, but choosing wrong.

"Anyone, then, who knows the good he ought to do and doesn't do it, sins." (James 4:17)

What is the major consequence of sin?

Spiritual death, which is spiritual separation from God.

"The wages of sin is death, but the gift of God is eternal life in Christ Jesus our Lord." (Romans 6:23)

#3 God's Provision for You is the *Savior.*

Can anything remove the penalty for sin?

Yes. Jesus died on the cross to personally pay the penalty for your sins.

"God demonstrates his own love for us in this: While we were still sinners, Christ died for us." (Romans 5:8)

What is the solution to being separated from God?

Acknowledging and believing in Jesus Christ as the only way to God the Father.

"Jesus answered, 'I am the way and the truth and the life. No one comes to the Father except through me.'" (John 14:6)

#4 Your Part is *Surrender.*

Place your faith in (rely on) Jesus Christ as your personal Lord and Savior and reject your "good works" as a means of gaining God's approval.

"It is by grace you have been saved, through faith—and this not from yourselves, it is the gift of God—not by works, so that no one can boast." (Ephesians 2:8–9)

Give Christ control of your life, entrusting yourself to Him.

"Jesus said to his disciples, 'If anyone would come after me, he must deny himself and take up his cross and follow me. For whoever wants to save his life will lose it, but whoever loses his life for me will find it. What good will it be for a man if he gains the whole world, yet forfeits his soul?'" (Matthew 16:24–26)

If you choose to believe in Him—place your faith in Him—*He will enable you to live the full, guilt-free life God desires for you.*

If you want to be fully forgiven by God—if you want to experience His mercy and grace by accepting Him as your personal Lord and Savior—you can tell Him in a simple, heartfelt prayer like this:

PRAYER OF SALVATION

"God, I want a real relationship with You.
I admit that many times
I've chosen to go my own way
instead of Your way.
I am genuinely grieved over my sins
and deeply regret them.
Jesus, thank You for dying on the cross
to pay the penalty for my sins.
Come into my life to be my Lord and my
Savior. Make me the person
You created me to be.
In Your holy name I pray. Amen."

What Can You Expect Now?

If you sincerely prayed the prayer of salvation, listen to what God says!

"Since we have been justified [vindicated—declared righteous] through faith, we have peace with God through our Lord Jesus Christ."
(Romans 5:1)

Having *"peace with God"* means that you have been brought into a good relationship with Him and you no longer need to grieve over your guilt because you are now forgiven.

WRONG BELIEFS:

▶ *Repressed Grief:*

"I should be able to handle the losses in my life without having to experience and work through deep pain and grief."

▶ *Chronic Grief:*

"My grief is more than I can bear. If I give in to it, I'm afraid it will consume me."

RIGHT BELIEF:

"Grief is a normal process that I must experience in order to grow emotionally and spiritually and to resolve my losses in life. My hope is in God, my Savior, who provides the strength for me to grieve deeply and honestly."

"My flesh and my heart may fail,
but God is the strength of my heart."
(Psalm 73:26)

STEPS TO SOLUTION

Each of us has experienced the grief of betrayal. Nothing wounds the heart more deeply than the betrayal of a trusted friend. Jesus understood the grief of betrayal, not just by one of his closest friends, but by two—Judas and Peter. These two disciples provide a vivid contrast between *godly sorrow* and *worldly sorrow*.

Both Judas and Peter grieved over the sickening reality of betraying Jesus. But Judas' betrayal resulted in further wrong choices. Overwhelmed with grief, Judas rushed headlong into *worldly sorrow*, and he ultimately committed suicide.

On the other hand, Peter's betrayal resulted in a *godly sorrow*. Rather than hardening his heart, Peter's godly sorrow led him to sincere repentance. This God-honoring repentance, in turn, led to Peter's complete reconciliation with Christ, and to a humble, yet powerful life that would forever impact the world.

Judas and Peter each had a choice. One chose death—the other chose life. As you face your season of grief, what will your choice be?

"Godly sorrow brings repentance that leads to salvation and leaves no regret, but worldly sorrow brings death."
(2 Corinthians 7:10)

Key Passage to Read and Reread

Jeremiah, known as *"the weeping prophet,"* authored the Book of Lamentations, in which he lamented ("cried aloud") over the destruction of Jerusalem and the Temple by the enemy. Jeremiah's lament is followed by his hope, which can be your hope when you feel like you are drowning in a sea of grief.

Lamentations 3:19–26

► God lifts me out of the sea of my downcast soul. (vv. 19–21)

► God's great love and compassion never fail. (v. 22)

► God's faithfulness comforts me daily. (v. 23)

► God is all I need. I will wait for Him. (v. 24)

► God wants all my hope to be placed only in Him. (v. 25)

► God is good to me when I seek Him. (v. 25)

► God brings healing as I wait for His deliverance. (v. 26)

Working through your grief will involve both your mind and your emotions.[15] Intellectually, you can know that a loss has occurred, but you can still emotionally refuse to accept how your life will be different because of that loss. The work of *accepting the reality* of your unwanted loss may consume all your energy, but your efforts will succeed when you have the right focus.

Rather than trying to feel what others want you to feel, focus on the Lord God. Pray, "Whatever You want me to feel and whatever You want me to do is my desire. My commitment is to be the person You want me to be through this season of sorrow."

> **"Whatever you do, work at it with all your heart, as working for the Lord, not for men." (Colossians 3:23)**

Accept Your Past

Accept that the past will always be in the past.

▶ *Pray.* Seek God's help in embracing your grief.

"The righteous cry out, and the Lord hears them; he delivers them from all their troubles. The Lord is close to the brokenhearted

and saves those who are crushed in spirit."
(Psalm 34:17–18)

▶ **Recall.** Think back on your loss, then write and finish these sentences.

- "I remember these significant events and memories ... " (<u>List both good and bad.</u>)

- "I look at these photographs and recall ..." (<u>List memories, good and bad.</u>)

- "I am grieving over ... " (<u>List all.</u>)

"Surely you desire truth in the inner parts; you teach me wisdom in the inmost place." (Psalm 51:6)

▶ **Weep.** Allow yourself to have tears.

"Weeping may remain for a night, but rejoicing comes in the morning." (Psalm 30:5)

▶ **Complete.** As you review, beside each event on your list, write the word *past*, which confirms, "I will be content to leave the past in the past."

"Godliness with contentment is great gain." (1 Timothy 6:6)

▶ **Memorize.** Write down these verses to memorize.

"My soul is weary with sorrow; strengthen me according to your word." (Psalm 119:28)

"My comfort in my suffering is this: Your promise preserves my life." (Psalm 119:50)

"I have suffered much; preserve my life, O LORD, according to your word." (Psalm 119:107)

"Your compassion is great, O LORD; preserve my life according to your laws." (Psalm 119:156)

▶ *Give thanks.* Thank God for all that He has taught you from the past and how He will use your past in the future. Pray, "God, Thank You for all that You have taught me from my past pain and how You will use that time of grief in my future."

"Give thanks in all circumstances, for this is God's will for you in Christ Jesus." (1 Thessalonians 5:18)

Accept Your Present

The present offers stability and significance.

▶ *Choose* to live one day at a time.

"Do not worry about tomorrow, for tomorrow will worry about itself. Each day has enough trouble of its own." (Matthew 6:34)

▶ *Put* the Lord at the center of your life.

"If anyone would come after me, he must deny

himself and take up his cross and follow me."
(Matthew 16:24)

▶ *Go* to God with your specific questions.
(Make a list.)

*"If any of you lacks wisdom, he should ask God,
who gives generously to all without finding
fault, and it will be given to him."* (James 1:5)

▶ *Thank* God for providing everything you
need for life.

*"His divine power has given us everything
we need for life and godliness through our
knowledge of him who called us by his own
glory and goodness."* (2 Peter 1:3)

▶ *Praise* God that though your situation has
changed, He will never leave you.

*"God has said, 'Never will I leave you; never
will I forsake you.'"* (Hebrews 13:5)

▶ *Focus* on the joy and satisfaction of helping
others. (Make a list.)

*"Carry each other's burdens, and in this
way you will fulfill the law of Christ."*
(Galatians 6:2)

Accept Your Future

The future affords new opportunities.

▶ *Hope* in the plans that God has for your future.

"'For I know the plans I have for you,' declares the LORD, 'plans to prosper you and not to harm you, plans to give you hope and a future.'" (Jeremiah 29:11)

▶ *Know* that your sorrow and grief will not be wasted.

"It was good for me to be afflicted so that I might learn your decrees." (Psalm 119:71)

▶ *Put* all your hope in God.

"Find rest, O my soul, in God alone; my hope comes from him." (Psalm 62:5)

▶ *Have* faith in God, whom you cannot see.

"We fix our eyes not on what is seen, but on what is unseen. For what is seen is temporary, but what is unseen is eternal." (2 Corinthians 4:18)

▶ *Know* that God will fill the void in your life.

"Forget the former things; do not dwell on the past. See, I am doing a new thing! Now it springs up; do you not perceive it? I am making a way in the desert and streams in the wasteland." (Isaiah 43:18–19)

Since grieving impacts us emotionally, physically, and spiritually, all three of these areas need to be considered when we go through the grieving process. If the following guidelines are taken to heart, the potentially harmful effects of grieving can be minimized, and the benefits can be maximized.

> "The prudent see danger
> and take refuge, but the simple
> keep going and suffer for it."
> (Proverbs 27:12)

Emotional Guidelines

▶ **Have a strong, sensitive support system.**

Having people around you who genuinely care about you is essential—people who accept you wherever you are in the grieving process and who encourage you to share your feelings with them.

"As iron sharpens iron, so one man sharpens another." (Proverbs 27:17)

▶ **Have the freedom to cry.**

Expressing emotions honestly, openly, and as frequently as needed is vital in order to walk through grief in a healthy, productive way.

"Those who sow in tears will reap with songs of joy." (Psalm 126:5)

▶ **Have a plan for socializing regularly.**

One of the helpful factors to feeling good about life, even while mourning, is attending social activities and interacting with others on a regular basis.

"Let us not give up meeting together, as some are in the habit of doing, but let us encourage one another." (Hebrews 10:25)

▶ **Have a trustworthy, honest confidante.**

Being able to be yourself with someone and share your struggles, your troubled thoughts, and swinging emotions—and then still to be accepted and affirmed—is healing to the soul.

"Two are better than one, because they have a good return for their work: If one falls down, his friend can help him up. But pity the man who falls and has no one to help him up!" (Ecclesiastes 4:9–10)

▶ **Have your resentment released.**

If you have unresolved issues, anger, or hostile feelings regarding your loss, take the time to list your resentments along with their causes. Journaling can bring to the surface buried emotions. Then release into the hands of God each offender and the pain of each offense.

"Be kind and compassionate to one another, forgiving each other, just as in Christ God forgave you." (Ephesians 4:32)

PRAYER

*"Lord, You know the pain
I have felt over (situations).
I release all that pain into Your hands
and, as an act of my will,
I choose to forgive (or release)
(person's name).
Thank You, Lord Jesus,
for setting me FREE."*

Physical Guidelines

BIBLICAL ILLUSTRATION:

Imagine a very real death threat on your life! Jezebel's edict had Elijah fleeing for his life, and he eventually collapsed beneath a tree. With intense grief over the possible loss of his own life, this godly prophet prayed that he would die. But God sent an angel with food and water. After Elijah ate and drank, he lay down again and rested. Later, the angel awakened him with more food and drink. With increased strength, Elijah was once again able to go on his way. (See 1 Kings 19:3–8.)

▶ **Get a sufficient amount of rest.**

Since grieving often disturbs regular sleep patterns and disrupts prolonged periods of sleeping, getting sufficient rest during the grieving process is often a challenge—but doing so is critically important to the body.

▶ **Get a generous intake of fluid.**

Because the sense of thirst is frequently unnoticed/undetected during the grieving process, drinking non-alcoholic and caffeine-free fluids is particularly important. Plenty of fluids are needed to carry away your body's toxic waste and to maintain appropriate electrolyte balance.

▶ **Get a balanced nutritional diet.**

Eat daily portions of food from each of the four basic food groups. Avoid skipping meals and consuming "junk" foods.

▶ **Get into a daily exercise routine.**

Regular exercise is a natural deterrent to feeling depressed and a natural means to feeling a sense of well-being. Exercise carries oxygen to the blood and promotes overall good health.

▶ **Get big doses of sunshine.**

Taking a walk in the sunshine is another natural way to fight depression. Light coming in through the eyes stimulates the brain to send a message to the body to release antidepressant endorphins.

"Light is sweet, and it pleases the eyes to see the sun." (Ecclesiastes 11:7)

Spiritual Guidelines

▶ **Develop a purposeful prayer life.**

The grieving process provides a strong impetus for "getting down to business" with God. Have candid conversations with Him about your thoughts and feelings. Listen to Him and lean on Him for comfort and reassurance.

"I recounted my ways and you answered me; teach me your decrees." (Psalm 119:26)

▶ Develop a yearning for eternity.

One of the most helpful, hopeful, and healing truths to realize is that this present life is being lived in a temporal body, but a permanent body is waiting for you. In that body you will live throughout all eternity. Grasp God's promise of living eternally!

"We do not lose heart. Though outwardly we are wasting away, yet inwardly we are being renewed day by day. For our light and momentary troubles are achieving for us an eternal glory that far outweighs them all. So we fix our eyes not on what is seen, but on what is unseen. For what is seen is temporary, but what is unseen is eternal." (2 Corinthians 4:16–18)

▶ Develop a positive, practical perspective.

Maintaining a positive mental attitude based on the practical application of spiritual truths during the grieving process will carry you to victory through the darkest valley and the deepest loss.

"Whatever is true, whatever is noble, whatever is right, whatever is pure, whatever is lovely, whatever is admirable—if anything is excellent or praiseworthy—think about such things." (Philippians 4:8)

▶ Develop a sense of peace about the past.

Resolve any unfinished business regarding the past by asking forgiveness of God for any failures on your part and by extending forgiveness for any failures on the part of others. Then let the past go and embrace the present and the future God has planned for you.

"If we confess our sins, he is faithful and just and will forgive us our sins and purify us from all unrighteousness." (1 John 1:9)

▶ Develop a Scripture memorization method.

God spoke the world into existence, and His written Word, the Bible, is powerful enough to create new life in you and to restore joy to your heart, peace to your mind, and hope for your future.

"All Scripture is God-breathed and is useful for teaching, rebuking, correcting and training in righteousness, so that the man of God may be thoroughly equipped for every good work." (2 Timothy 3:16–17)

The prophet Samuel apparently had difficulty letting go of his grief over his beloved King Saul after Saul had violated God's directives so grievously that God rejected him as king.

> **"Until the day Samuel died,**
> **he did not go to see Saul again,**
> **though Samuel mourned for him....**
> **The Lord said to Samuel,**
> **'How long will you mourn for Saul?'"**
> **(1 Samuel 15:35; 16:1)**

Many who are grieving never get over the final hurdle of letting go of the pain and saying goodbye. One method of accomplishing this task is to place an empty chair in front of you and imagine in the chair is whatever or whoever was lost to you, ready to hear and accept whatever you need to say.

For the woman grieving over the childhood sexual abuse in her past, this may mean imagining her abuser across from her and then verbalizing her feelings about what was done to her and coming to some resolve regarding those feelings, forgiving the offender, releasing her pain to God, and moving her focus from the past to the present.

For the man who has lost his wife, this may mean verbalizing to her any unresolved feelings about her life or her death. By expressing his feelings as well as his need to move on with his life, he then says a final farewell to her and to their marriage. This act may need to be repeated until there is true relief through letting go, saying goodbye, and embracing the future as a whole person again.

> "He heals the brokenhearted
> and binds up their wounds."
> (Psalm 147:3)

Letting Go

▶ *Look back* and verbally reflect on the history you have shared with that which is lost. Acknowledge that history as a permanent part of your past but no longer a part of your present.

▶ *Express* any unfinished business regarding the past and resolve any remaining issues or feelings (such as regrets or resentments), emptying them out and bringing them to closure.

▶ *Choose* to forgive whatever grievances you may still be harboring and let go of any thoughts of revenge.

▶ *Release* the past to the past and commit to cease trying to make it a part of your present and your future. Relegate the past to the past, letting it go and leaving it there. Allow these words from the Book of Job to reflect the disposition of your heart.

"You will surely forget your trouble, recalling it only as waters gone by." (Job 11:16)

Saying Goodbye

▶ ***Look back*** and reflect on the significance of the history you have shared with that which has been lost, exploring and expressing the depth and breadth of your feelings (such as love, appreciation, anger, and guilt).

▶ ***Acknowledge*** the impact your history has had on you as a person. Accept the fact that it will always be a part of who you are. But affirm also that it is time for you to move on with your life and become the person God is making of you *now*.

▶ ***State*** that you cannot live in the past and that you have present needs that God plans to meet in new ways. Acknowledge that you need to embrace all that God has for you.

▶ ***Say goodbye*** to the past and to the pain and to all that has been lost. Express your final sentiments that need to be said and say, "Goodbye." Then turn your focus to the present and to the future that God has already planned for you, embracing your life now and your life as it will be in the future. Realize that you are ever in process and, therefore, ever changing. Say hello to whatever Jesus has for your life now.

"Peace I leave with you; my peace I give you. I do not give to you as the world gives. Do not let your hearts be troubled and do not be afraid." (John 14:27)

FINDING Comfort

How true the saying, "All sunshine makes a desert." God knows that if you never experience the storms of life—if the rain clouds never release their water—you will never see flower gardens grow. You need to blossom in the areas of sympathy, empathy, and compassion, understanding, perspective, and wisdom. Our God is the God of the second chance. Whatever is in the past can be used for God's glory. The storms of sorrow should never be wasted. By God's design, grief will better your heart and life. Grief will make you grow.

> **"Sorrow is better than laughter, because a sad face is good for the heart." (Ecclesiastes 7:3)**

▶ **Come to the God of all comfort.**

"Praise be to the God and Father of our Lord Jesus Christ, the Father of compassion and the God of all comfort." (2 Corinthians 1:3)

▶ **Open your heart to the reality of pain.**

"Indeed, in our hearts we felt the sentence of death. But this happened that we might not rely on ourselves but on God, who raises the dead." (2 Corinthians 1:9)

▶ **Maintain a clear conscience by confessing past sins and offenses.**

"He who conceals his sins does not prosper, but whoever confesses and renounces them finds mercy." (Proverbs 28:13)

▶ **Find the positive in your grief process.**

"See what this godly sorrow has produced in you: what earnestness, what eagerness to clear yourselves, what indignation, what alarm, what longing, what concern, what readiness to see justice done. At every point you have proved yourselves to be innocent in this matter." (2 Corinthians 7:11)

▶ **Obtain comfort from those whom God will send to you.**

"God, who comforts the downcast, comforted us by the coming of Titus." (2 Corinthians 7:6)

▶ **Reinforce your faith by giving comfort to others.**

"[God] comforts us in all our troubles, so that we can comfort those in any trouble with the comfort we ourselves have received from God." (2 Corinthians 1:4)

▶ **Trust in the strength of Christ in you for the power to rebuild your life.**

"I can do everything through him who gives me strength." (Philippians 4:13)

PRAYER

"Just as the farther you are from a flower,
the smaller it seems to your eyes;
so, the farther your distance from grief,
the smaller your sadness in sorrow.
Time indeed is a healer—
a gift of comfort from the God
of all comfort.

—*June Hunt*

Grieving over Loss of a Godly Parent

QUESTION: "Ever since the death of my godly dad, I've been angry with God and have turned away from the church. How can I get over my grief and face the future without my father?"

ANSWER: The loss of a godly parent can be severely painful. Instead of focusing solely on how much you miss him ...

▶ Focus on what would bring honor to his memory.

▶ Ask yourself, "If my dad were still alive, what would give him the greatest joy?"

Based on the Bible, your dad's greatest joy would be for you to follow in his footsteps, to live a Christlike life and to grow in the truths of God.

> "I have no greater joy than to hear
> that my children are
> walking in the truth."
> (3 John 1:4)

Grieving over Unforgiveness

QUESTION: "Someone close to me died, and now it is too late for me to ask forgiveness for what I did wrong. What can I do about my heavy guilt?"

ANSWER: You do not have to live with guilt even though the person you wronged is no longer available to you.

Realize that God is available to you.

▶ Write down every wrong attitude and action and then confess your sin to Him.

▶ Ask God's forgiveness, realizing that all sins (even against others) are sins against God because He has told us how we are to treat one another.

▶ Write a letter to the one you wronged, read it aloud, and ask God to forgive you on behalf of the other person.

God knows your heart, and He can forgive your sins and restore to you a clear conscience.

"Create in me a pure heart, O God,
and renew a steadfast spirit within me....
The sacrifices of God are a broken spirit;
a broken and contrite heart,
O God, you will not despise."
(Psalm 51:10, 17)

Grieving: Life Not Back to Normal

QUESTION: "I have experienced a devastating death in my family, and nothing feels the same. Everyone keeps telling me that things will get back to normal, but are they right?"

ANSWER: When death takes someone dear to your heart, your life will not "get back to normal." However, you will need to establish a *"new normal."* When your life is forever changed by a life-altering loss, your *"old normal"* vanishes forever. Yet, as you settle into a *new routine* with a *new mindset*, you will develop a *new normal*—and over time, your comfort level will increase. During this process, remember that:

▶ God made you to be resilient by equipping you to adapt mentally, emotionally, and spiritually to new situations.

▶ Life itself consists of never-ending change from the moment of conception to the moment of death.

▶ We are forever changing and being given the opportunity to grow in maturity with each new change.

Trust the Lord, who created you, and lean on Him as you find your "new normal."

"Trust in the LORD with all your heart and lean not on your own understanding; in all your ways acknowledge him, and he will make your paths straight."
(Proverbs 3:5–6)

Grieving: Dealing with Anger toward God

QUESTION: "I have immense anger toward God for taking my child from me when she was the joy and the delight of my life. Why did God take her?"

ANSWER: Any significant loss results in grief. However, one of the most severe losses is the loss of a child. The natural order in life deems that children outlive their parents, not the reverse. Certainly God understands your anguish, and He can shoulder your anger. In order to overcome your anger at God:

▶ Honestly share your feelings with Him.

▶ Ask Him to give you insight into His heart for you and His plan now for your life.

▶ Realize the heavenly Father is also a parent and that He has the heart of a parent toward you.

▶ Trust that God is perfect in His love for you and for your cherished daughter.

▶ Thank God for every moment He allowed you to spend with your daughter.

▶ Realize that your daughter has not been lost to you forever. She will spend eternity with you after God's time for you here on earth is complete.

▶ Focus on what will honor your daughter's memory as you live your life.

This grief in your life has not come from a heart of stone, but from a heart of love and compassion. While you may not see it now, God does not find pleasure in bringing grief to His beloved children, but He does what He does from His position as the sovereign, all-knowing, all-loving God.

"Though he brings grief, he will show compassion, so great is his unfailing love. For he does not willingly bring affliction or grief to the children of men." (Lamentations 3:32–33)

Grieving: Dealing with Anniversary Depression

QUESTION: "Every year for the past several years I have become depressed during the time of the year when my husband died. Why is it happening, and what can I do to stop it?"

ANSWER: You are experiencing what is commonly referred to as "Anniversary Depression," a yearly recurring reaction to a past loss or trauma. This involuntary depression correlates to the anniversary date of your loss and lasts for a limited period of time. Since you know the time period of your recurring depression, you might plan ahead of time to process some of your grief with a wise, caring friend or counselor. And, since the depression is triggered by conscious or unconscious memories, you can choose to create new memories around that date, such as these:

▶ planning a trip with someone special around the time of the anniversary

▶ going to a Christian seminar or workshop to help keep your focus on the Lord and on His healing Word

▶ attending a social event so you will not be alone or inviting loved ones for dinner at your home

▶ giving loved ones a special remembrance in your husband's honor (a poem, a picture, or a possession that belonged to him)

▶ initiating a project in honor of his life

"The memory of the righteous
will be a blessing."
(Proverbs 10:7)

Grieving: Feeling Guilty because of Tears

QUESTION: "I have had a major loss in my life but I should be over it by now. Why can't I stop crying and, at times, why do I cry for no apparent reason? I feel so guilty about my tears."

ANSWER: There is no timetable for when you should be "over" grieving a significant loss. Losses are not to be "gotten over." Our losses should be accepted, and our lives should be adjusted to accommodate our losses in such a way that the quality of our lives is not lessened, but is instead enriched. This can be a reality for you because God promises to use all things for good in the lives of those who love Him (Romans 8:28). As you go through the grief process, remember:

▶ Tears may come sporadically for years after your loss whenever something consciously or unconsciously reminds you of your loss.

▶ A smell, a place, a song, a person, or any number of things can trigger stored unconscious memories.

▶ Rather than trying to control your reactions, let them come freely, and you will find that by experiencing them they will dissipate over time.

▶ Tears are for a reason, and they are for a season. They are the body's way of releasing deep emotional, physical, mental, and spiritual pain. When the pain is released, the tears subside.

Those who love deeply, cry freely at the loss of the object of their love. Good for you for loving deeply! You are like God in that way, for He loves deeply too.

"I have loved you with an everlasting love; I have drawn you with loving-kindness." (Jeremiah 31:3)

Grieving: Dealing with a Most Difficult Time

QUESTION: "It has been almost six months since my loved one died, and instead of getting better, I seem to be getting worse. What is wrong with me?"

ANSWER: The truth is nothing is wrong with you. Your grieving is right on schedule. Although many people are not aware of it, the sixth month after the loss of a loved one is generally the worst period of time. It is like an unexpected second tidal wave has struck you and sent you reeling right when you thought you might be getting somewhat of a handle on your grief. As you deal with this second wave of grief, realize:

▶ What happens at six months is that reality sets in on a much deeper level and opens up more of your soul to acknowledge and accept the significance of your loss.

▶ God does much of His work in us through a period of time rather than instantaneously.

You are in the grief process. While you are presently experiencing great sorrow, that sorrow will complete its work in you, and you will find that it has carved out within you a deep well that God, in His time, will fill with joy and peace and contentment.

"May the God of hope fill you with all joy
and peace as you trust in him,
so that you may overflow with hope
by the power of the Holy Spirit."
(Romans 15:13)

Grieving: Dealing with Decisions

QUESTION: "I recently lost my husband, and I feel like I am in a dense, heavy fog and cannot see my way out of it. I know there are some major decisions I need to make about what to do with the house and whether I should stay in it or sell it and move somewhere else. What should I do?"

ANSWER: Your feelings are completely normal and totally understandable given your situation.

The death of a spouse is highly distressing and generally leaves the survivor in a state of shock for days or weeks and disoriented for months. Therefore, the most commonly given advice to recent widows and widowers is that no major decisions or changes should be made for at least a year. Consider:

► The task of going through the grief process is a big enough job during that first year and maybe even longer.

► Unless you are under some time constraints, delay making any major decisions and any significant life changes for another year or so—a time when you will be less stressed and better able to think clearly about the pros and cons of such decisions.

► Right now you don't know where you will want to live in a year or two or what you will want to pursue.

The bottom line is that waiting to make a big decision until you know that you will not regret it later is the best thing to do.

"I will instruct you and teach you
in the way you should go;
I will counsel you and watch over you."
(Psalm 32:8)

QUESTION: "People keep asking me to socialize with them, but I don't want to be around anyone—I don't want to try to have fun or make conversation. Why can't people understand that in my grief, I just want to be left alone?"

ANSWER: People do understand your desire for isolation, and that is precisely why they are concerned about your being alone too much. Becoming self-absorbed, losing interest in socializing, and desiring to isolate yourself from others are common when you are in the grief process. However, there is also potential danger of becoming a recluse to the point that you become stuck in your grief and fail to reach out to others in an effort to stay connected to life apart from sorrow. One of the most effective ways to help your own healing is to reach out to others who are grieving.

▶ Identify with the grief of others.

▶ Be available as someone who can understand how they feel.

▶ Send a card, prepare a meal, bring a flower, run an errand.

▶ Make periodic phone calls to say, "I care."

Remember that isolating from others only

curtails your own healing. Instead, reaching out will help bring healing to others and, in turn, to yourself.

> "A generous man will prosper;
> he who refreshes others
> will himself be refreshed."
> (Proverbs 11:25)

Grieving the Holy Spirit

QUESTION: "I feel horrible guilt and huge grief. Although I'm a Christian, I've gone against God, and now the damage has been done. Can I ever have peace again with God?"

ANSWER: When you have unresolved sin, you *should* feel unresolved grief. Why? Because you have actually *grieved the Holy Spirit*! Realize that, because you are an authentic Christian, the Spirit of God resides within you. Therefore:

▶ When you are in the will of God, you have peace with God (one aspect of the "fruit of the Spirit").

▶ When you are not in the will of God, you will not have peace with God. The reason the Holy Spirit removed His peace from you was to convict you of sin so that you would correct your course. Do what pleases God, and you will have the peace of God.

> "Do not grieve the Holy Spirit of God."
> (Ephesians 4:30)

When someone experiences a devastating loss, God most often uses the comfort and encouragement of others to bring healing. As you reach out to others with the compassion of Christ, consider the following helpful hints for building others up when they are in the midst of grief.

▶ Acknowledge their loss immediately.

▶ Accept all emotional or verbal responses without judging them.

▶ Hug with tender affection.

▶ Expect tears and emotional extremes.

▶ Find helpful things to do without being asked.

▶ Give the one grieving many opportunities to talk about the loss.

> "Encourage one another
> and build each other up."
> (1 Thessalonians 5:11)

▶ DEATH OF A CHILD

Don't say, "You can always have another child."

Do say, "I appreciated your special qualities as a mother to your child."

▶ DEATH OF A SPOUSE

Don't say, "A lot of people remarry at your age."

Do say, "I valued his/her (character trait or ability)."

▶ DEATH AFTER A LONG ILLNESS

Don't say, "She's so much better off now."

Do say, "I admire the way you encouraged and helped her."

▶ DIVORCE OR SEPARATION

Don't say, "He was never good enough for you."

Do say, "The Lord is here for you, and I will also be here for you."

▶ DISABLED CHILD

Don't say, "Was there something you did to cause the handicap?"

Do say, "I noticed your child's (sweet disposition, nice smile)."

▶ LOSS OF JOB

Don't say, "You'll find a better job within a week."

Do say, "I feel for you and will pray with you during this time."

▶ LOSS OF LIMB

Don't say, "Be thankful—you could have died."

Do say, "The adjustment will be difficult, but you can do it. Count on me to be of help."

▶ **LOSS OF HOUSE**

Don't say, "At least you're still alive."

Do say, "I know you have many memories in your home. I remember ... "

▶ **LOSS OF PET**

Don't say, "You can always get another pet."

Do say, "You were so good to your dog."

▶ **LOSS OF FRIEND**

Don't say, "You'll make other good friends."

Do say, "A friend is a treasure. I know you will miss him/her"

▶ **LOSS AS A RESULT OF ANY TRAGEDY**

Don't say, "All things work together for good!" (even though that is ultimately true)

Do say, "Although I don't know why this happened to you, I do know the Lord will stay close to you. One particular Scripture that helped me is Psalm 34:18, '*The LORD is close to the brokenhearted and saves those who are crushed in spirit.*'"

"A word aptly spoken is like
apples of gold in settings of silver."
(Proverbs 25:11)

SCRIPTURES TO MEMORIZE

Does anyone **see** my **trouble and grief**?

*"You, O God, do **see trouble and grief**; you consider it to take it in hand. The victim commits himself to you."* (Psalm 10:14)

Who can **I call for help**?

*"O LORD my God, **I called** to you **for help** and you healed me."* (Psalm 30:2)

How can I **find rest** for **my soul**?

*"**Find rest**, O **my soul**, in God alone; my hope comes from him."* (Psalm 62:5)

How long will my **weeping remain**?

*"**Weeping** may **remain** for a night, but rejoicing comes in the morning."* (Psalm 30:5)

How can I stop feeling so **downcast** and **disturbed** within my soul?

*"Why are you **downcast**, O my soul? Why so **disturbed** within me? Put your hope in God, for I will yet praise him, my Savior and my God."* (Psalm 42:11)

Can my **broken heart** ever **heal**?

*"He **heals** the **brokenhearted** and binds up their wounds."* (Psalm 147:3)

Can I have any **consolation** with **my unrelenting pain?**

*"I would still have this **consolation**—**my joy** in **unrelenting pain**—that I had not denied the words of the Holy One."* (Job 6:10)

How can I not **dwell on the past?**

*"Forget the former things; **do not dwell on the past**. See, I am doing a new thing! Now it springs up; do you not perceive it? I am making a way in the desert and streams in the wasteland."* (Isaiah 43:18–19)

What happens when **God comforts us in all our troubles?**

*"The Father of compassion and the God of all comfort ... **comforts us in all our troubles**, so that we can comfort those in any trouble with the comfort we ourselves have received from God."* (2 Corinthians 1:3–4)

Will my **grief** ever **turn to joy?**

*"You will weep and mourn while the world rejoices. You will grieve, but your **grief will turn to joy**."* (John 16:20)

NOTES

1. John A. Larson, "Grief," in *Baker Encyclopedia of Psychology & Counseling*, 2d ed., ed. David G. Benner and Peter C. Hill (Grand Rapids: Baker, 1999), 519.

2. James Strong, *Strong's Exhaustive Concordance of the Bible* (Nashville: Abingdon, 1986), 45.

3. Strong, *Strong's Exhaustive Concordance of the Bible*, 7.

4. Gary R. Collins, *Christian Counseling: A Comprehensive Guide*, rev. ed. (Dallas: Word, 1988), 352–53; H. Norman Wright, *Crisis Counseling: What to Do and Say During the First 72 Hours*, updated and expanded ed. (Ventura, CA: Regal, 1993), 154–56; H. Norman Wright, *Recovering from the Losses of Life* (Tarrytown, NY: Fleming H. Revell, 1991), 53–61.

5. Collins, *Christian Counseling*, 352–53; Wright, *Crisis Counseling*, 154–56; Wright, *Recovering from the Losses of Life*, 53–61.

6. Charlotte A. Greeson, Mary Hollingsworth, and Michael Washburn, *The Grief Adjustment Guide: A Pathway through Pain*, Faire & Hale Planner (Sisters, OR: Questar, 1990), 200–2.

7. Wright, *Crisis Counseling*, 158–59.

8. Wright, *Crisis Counseling*, 159–61.

9. Greeson, Hollingsworth, and Washburn, *The Grief Adjustment Guide*, 73; Wright, *Crisis Counseling*, 165.

10. Collins, *Christian Counseling*, 352–53; Wright, *Crisis Counseling*, 154–56; Wright, *Recovering from the Losses of Life*, 53–61.

11. Haddon W. Robinson, *Grief: Comfort for Those Who Grieve and Those Who Want to Help* (Grand Rapids: Discovery House, 1996), 11–16.

12. Lawrence J. Crabb, Jr., *Understanding People: Deep Longings for Relationship*, Ministry Resources Library (Grand Rapids: Zondervan, 1987), 15–16; Robert S. McGee, *The Search for Significance*, 2nd ed. (Houston, TX: Rapha, 1990), 27–30.

13. Adapted from Glen W. Davidson, *Understanding Mourning: A Guide For Those Who Grieve* (Minneapolis, MN: Augsburg Publishing House, 1984), 15–19.

14. Joel A. Freeman, *God Is Not Fair* (San Bernardino, CA: Here's Life, 1987), 130–34.

15. Wright, *Crisis Counseling*, 159.

SELECTED BIBLIOGRAPHY

Briggs, Lauren. *What You Can Say When You Don't Know What to Say.* Eugene, OR: Harvest House, 1985.

Collins, Gary R. *Christian Counseling: A Comprehensive Guide.* Rev. ed. Dallas: Word, 1988.

Crabb, Lawrence J., Jr. *Understanding People: Deep Longings for Relationship.* Ministry Resources Library. Grand Rapids: Zondervan, 1987.

Davidson, Glen W. *Understanding Mourning: A Guide for Those Who Grieve.* Minneapolis: Augsburg, 1984.

Freeman, Joel A. *God Is Not Fair.* San Bernardino, CA: Here's Life, 1987.

Greeson, Charlotte A., Mary Hollingsworth, and Michael Washburn. *The Grief Adjustment Guide: A Pathway through Pain.* Faire & Hale Planner. Sisters, OR: Questar, 1990.

Kreeft, Peter and Ronald K. Tacelli. *Handbook of Christian Apologetics.* Downers Grove, IL: InterVarsity, 1994.

Larson, John A. "Grief." In *Baker Encyclopedia of Psychology & Counseling*, 2d ed, edited by David G. Benner and Peter C. Hill. Grand Rapids: Baker, 1999.

McGee, Robert S. *The Search for Significance: Book & Workbook*. 2d ed. Houston, TX: Rapha, 1990.

Rhea, Carolyn. *When Grief Is Your Constant Companion: God's Grace for a Woman's Heartache*. Birmingham, AL: New Hope, 2003.

Robinson, Haddon W. *Grief: Comfort for Those Who Grieve and Those Who Want to Help*. Grand Rapids: Discovery House, 1996.

Strong, James. *Strong's Exhaustive Concordance of the Bible*. Nashville: Abingdon, 1986.

West, Kari. *Dare to Trust, Dare to Hope Again: Living with Losses of the Heart*. Colorado Springs, CO: Cook Communications, 2001.

Westberg, Granger E. *Good Grief: A Constructive Approach to the Problem of Loss*. Philadelphia, PA: Fortress, 1962.

Wiersbe, Warren W. *Why Us? When Bad Things Happen to God's People*. Old Tappan, NJ: Fleming H. Revell, 1984.

Wright, H. Norman. *Crisis Counseling: What to Do and Say During the First 72 Hours*. Updated and expanded ed. Ventura, CA: Regal, 1993.

Wright, H. Norman. *Recovering from the Losses of Life*. Tarrytown, NY: Fleming H. Revell, 1991.

June Hunt's HOPE FOR THE HEART minibooks are biblically-based, and full of practical advice that is relevant, spiritually-fulfilling and wholesome.

HOPE FOR THE HEART TITLES

www.aspirepress.com

The HOPE FOR THE HEART Biblical Counseling Library is Your Solution!

- Easy-to-read, perfect for anyone.
- Short. Only 96 pages. Good for the busy person.
- Christ-centered biblical advice and practical help
- Tested and proven over 20 years of June Hunt's radio ministry
- 30 titles in the series – each tackling a key issue people face today.
- Affordable. You or your church can give away, lend, or sell them.

Display available for churches and ministries.

www.aspirepress.com